MEN-AT-ARMS SERIES

EDITOR: MARTIN WINDROW

The Apaches

Text by JASON HOOK

Colour plates by RICHARD HOOK

OSPREY PUBLISHING LONDON

Published in 1987 by
Osprey Publishing Ltd
Member company of the George Philip Group
12–14 Long Acre, London WC2E 9LP
© Copyright 1987 Osprey Publishing Ltd

British Library Cataloguing in Publication Data

Hook, Jason
    The Apaches.—(Men-at-arms series; 186)
    1. Apache Indians—History
    I. Title   II. Series
    970.004'97   E99.A6

    ISBN 0-85045-738-6

Filmset in Great Britain
Printed through Bookbuilders Ltd, Hong Kong

Acknowledgements
Special thanks to the Arizona State Museum,
University of Arizona. Thanks also to Ian Ford,
Badger and Dawn Kirby, Robin May, Bill Merklein,
Moose and Lizzie Wells, and Ian M. West.

Introduction

he origin of the name 'Apache' is unclear, though probably stems from the Zuni '*ápachu*', their name r the Navajo, who the early Spaniards called Apaches de Nabaju'. One suggested alternative is at it originated in the rare Spanish spelling pache' of 'mapache', meaning raccoon, which in ew of the distinctive white stripes typically aubed across a warrior's face is rather attractive, if likely. The Apaches in fact referred to themselves ith variants of '*ndé*', simply meaning, in common ith many Indian self-designations, 'the people'.

The Apache culture of 1850 was a blend of fluences from the peoples of the Great Plains, reat Basin and the South-West, particularly the ueblos, and—as time progressed—from the panish and American settlers. Tribal peculiarities pended upon geographical location in relation to ese peoples, and the time and route of a tribe's rly migration. In a work of this size, general-ations concerning 'typical' Apache traits of the hiricahua, Mescalero, Jicarilla, Western and pan Apaches—e.g. the eating of mescal, hunting d gathering economy, the puberty rite, masked npersonators of the Mountain Spirit pernaturals—inevitably have to be made. Tribal d indeed individual divergences naturally occur-d in what was a highly individualistic society; but here a reference is made to a *common* trait, it scribes a feature considered integral to the rich d distinctive Apachean culture.

1880s studio shot of Nalté, a San Carlos Apache warrior, pelled the 'San Carlos dude'. Note the identification tag nging from his necklace, and the quirt on a thong around his ·ist. The Frank Wesson carbine he is holding is a studio prop. rizona State Museum, University of Arizona)

The Apache Tribes

The Apachean or Southern Athapaskan language, and therefore the Apache people themselves, can be divided into seven tribal groups: Navajo, Western, Chiricahua, Mescalero, Jicarilla, Lipan, and Kiowa-Apache. For the purposes of this work, the **Navajo**, because they came to be considered as a distinct entity by virtue of developments in their culture, must be excluded. (While they are always regarded as a distinct tribe, their Apachean origins are nevertheless reflected in striking similarities to certain Apache traits.)

Of the six true Apache tribes, the **Kiowa-Apache** were the least integrated into Apache society. The earliest known divergence in language, *c.*AD1300, occurred between the Western and Kiowa-Apache, the latter separating from the other Apache groups before the beginnings of influence from the Pueblos of the South-West. The Kiowa-Apache remained on the north-eastern fringes of the South-West, and had no historic political con-

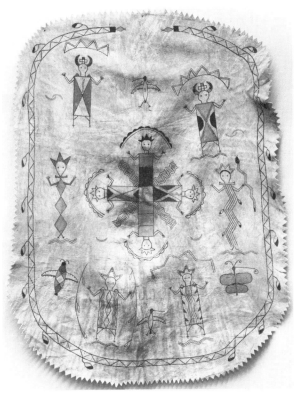

A shaman's painted buckskin, embellished with designs invoking supernatural power for curing ceremonies. (Arizona State Museum, University of Arizona)

nections with the Apaches. They adopted instead Plains-orientated culture, closely related, as the name suggests, to the Kiowa Indians. Whil retaining their own identity the Kiowa-Apach despite their alien language and origin, formed component part of the Kiowa camp-circle an society.

The Apache tribes most closely related to th Kiowa-Apache were the **Lipan**, who had a lesse degree of Plains influence in their culture. They ha a weakly developed band organisation, reportedl consisting of three bands in the early 19th centur These bands probably corresponded to th Lipanjenne, Lipanes de Arriba and Lipanes Aba described by Orozco y Berra (1864).

Jicarilla

The closest relations of the Lipan were the Jicaril Apache, whose mountainous territory ranged fro north-eastern New Mexico into southern Colorad The Jicarilla, whose name comes from the Spanis 'little basket' in reference to the women's experti in basket-weaving, numbered about 800 in 185 They were divided into two bands. Those west the Rio Grande were known as '*saidindê*', 'sar people', and comprised six local groups. They we also known by the Spanish name Ollerc 'potters'—although, as they were a mounta people, it has been suggested that this should Hoyeros, 'people of the mountain dells'. The eig local groups east of the Rio Grande were t '*gulgahén*' or Llaneros, meaning 'plains peopl They comprised, at least in part, the Plains Apac group referred to as Lipiyanes, whose Cuartale Paloma and Carlena bands were absorbed into t Jicarilla after 1800. While there was no linguistic cultural division between the eastern and weste bands, membership depending simply on residenc there was a strong two-band consciousness. T competitiveness between the moieties, best illu trated by the annual ceremonial relay race, w similar to that of the northern Pueblos of the R Grande.

Mescalero

South of the Jicarilla Apache were the Mescaler The name is a Spanish term meaning 'mesc makers': a reference to their extensive use of t agave or century mescal plant which made important contribution to Apache subsistence. The Mescalero lived among the Sacramento, Guadalupe and Davis Mountains of south-east New Mexico and western Texas, their homeland centring on the forbidding 12,000-foot peak of Sierra Blanca. Their hunting range spread south into Mexico, and east of the Pecos River on to the Plains. The Mescalero were loosely divided into the *gulgahénde*', 'people of the Plains', east of the mountains; and the *'ni't'áhende'*, 'earth crevice people', living in the mountains. Tribal culture was, however, uniform throughout, and this purely geographical division had no definite boundaries or function. Organisation into bands was weakly developed, most bands being known by the name of the mountain range that they occupied. The main Mescalero band were the Sierra Blanca, while the Apache group known as the Faraones made up a southern division. Band territories were poorly defined, just as they were among the other buffalo-hunting Apache tribes. This was perhaps dictated, in the case of the Mescalero, by the fact that buffalo herds roamed only in the eastern lowlands; so only with a fluid system of weakly defined bands and boundaries could tribesmen from other parts of the Mescalero range share in this vital resource.

Chiricahua

Division into bands was far more important to the Chiricahua, probably the most famous Apache tribe. They were divided into three bands, each with minor cultural differences. A confusing variety of ambiguous names have been used to denote various parts of the Chiricahua, but the band divisions can be simplified as follows.

The Eastern Chiricahua inhabited territory in south-west New Mexico, west of the Rio Grande. Their Chiricahua name was *'čihéne'* meaning 'red paint people', because of the red band typically daubed across their faces. The term Gileños or Gila Apaches was used at different times by the Spaniards to denote various groups. It specifically denoted, however, those Apaches living at the headwaters of the Gila River, and can be treated as synonymous with the Eastern Chiricahua. The Eastern Chiricahua or Gileños were, after 1800, identified as containing two distinct groups: the Mimbres and the Mogollon Apaches, each named after the mountain ranges they inhabited. The

Naiché, son of Cochise of the Central Chiricahua, 1880. He wears a magnificent owl-feather war-cap which invoked supernatural power for swiftness and protection in battle. (**Arizona State Museum, University of Arizona**)

Mimbres or Mimbreños were also known as Coppermine Apaches, and were at times divided into two closely related groups, known as the Coppermine (Mimbres) Apaches and the Warm Springs (Ojo Caliente) Apaches.

While Geronimo's people, the Bedonkohe Apaches, have sometimes been referred to as a distinct tribe, its seems likely that they were identical with the Mogollon Apaches. Thus, the Eastern Chiricahua band (Gileños) comprised the Mimbreños (Coppermine or Mimbres, and Warm Springs Apaches) and Mogollon (Bedonkohe) Apache groups.

The second Chiricahua band were the Chokonens, also known as the central or true Chiricahua and the Cochise Apaches, after their renowned leader. Their lands stretched into Mexico and New Mexico from south-east Arizona's Chiricahua

5

White Mountain Apache scouts, with Gen. George Crook in the background in his distinctive white pith helmet. Note the Plains-like shield hung with eagle feathers held by a scout in the foreground. The date is uncertain, being either mid-1870s or mid-1880s. (Arizona State Museum, University of Arizona)

Mountains, which gave the band and the tribe their name, and which contained the infamous Apache Pass.

South of the true Chiricahua were the third and final band, the Southern Chiricahua, who ranged the Sierra Madre region of northern Mexico. They were known as the Nednhi, 'enemy people', and were sometimes referred to, in part or whole, as Pinery or Bronco Apaches.

Western Apache

North of the Chiricahua tribe were the Western Apache of Arizona, who were, in the 1800s, divided into five autonomous groups based on slight differences in dialect.

The easternmost and largest group were the White Mountain Apache, whose lands stretched from the Pinaleño Mountains in the south to the White Mountains in the north. They were divided into the Eastern White Mountain and Western White Mountain bands, and sometimes referred to as Coyoteros. An earlier division into the Sierra Blanca (White Mountain) in the north and Coyotero in the south has been suggested.

To the north of the White Mountain Apache

were the Cibecue group, whose lands reached we north of the Mogollon Rim, skirted to the west b the Sierra Ancha. The Cibecue contained th Carrizo, Cibecue and Canyon Creek bands. To th south-west were the San Carlos group, roaming th foothills of the Galuiro and Santa Catalin Mountains. They comprised the San Carlo Apache Peaks, Pinal and Arivaipa bands, the la two possibly originating in the absorption of distinc Pinaleños and Arivaipa Apaches. Because th language of the San Carlos group was used in earl studies, their name is sometimes applied to all th Western Apache.

To the north-west were the Northern an Southern Tonto groups. The Southern Tonto ranging north from the Sierra Ancha and Mazatz; mountains, were divided into the Mazatzal ban and six unnamed semi-bands. The Northern Tonto who lived just south of the San Francisc mountains, contained the Bald Mountain, Foss Creek, Mormon Lake and Oak Creek bands. Th Tonto groups, particularly the Northern Tonto were very closely related to the Yuman tribe calle the Yavapais. The name Tonto was used to deno the south-eastern Yavapais, and it is thought tha the Tonto divisions of the Western Apache ma have originated in intermarriage between thes Indians and Apaches. While the division of th Tonto Apaches into northern and southern grou s an integral part of Goodwin's authoritative interpretation of Western Apache society, the Tontos always regarded themselves as a single group.

Various names have been applied to all or parts of the Western Apache. They have been referred to collectively as Tontos, though this term in its widest sense was usually applied to those Yuman and Apache groups occupying the Tonto Basin. The term 'Pinaleños' has been used as a major division of the Western Apache, but usually refers to those Indians roaming the Pinal Mountains. Both the entire Western Apache tribe and the White Mountain division have been described as Coyoteros.

The Apache tribes can be divided into three groups according to language, and to the time of migration into the historic area. The Western Apache, Mescalero and Chiricahua form what can be described as the typical Apache group, to which the Navajo originally belonged. The second group comprises the Jicarilla and Lipan, and the third the Kiowa-Apache. Cultural distinctions among the Apache conform with these divisions to a certain degree, those tribes living in close contact with each other sharing certain traits. Thus there were close

links between the Chiricahua and Mescalero, who were the last tribes to assume separate identities.

The geographical position of the tribes similarly affected their culture, through the influence of non-Apachean tribes and contact with the people of the South-West, Plains and Great Basin. Where generalisations are made about the Apache tribes as a whole, the Kiowa-Apache, by virtue of their strong affiliation with the Plains, tend to deviate severely from the norm, and should not be considered.

Apache Life

Social Structure

The social structure of the Apache people followed a typical pattern. The Apache population was thinly spread, scattered into relatively small groups across large tribal territories. Such an existence in a harsh environment did not lend itself to a regimented social structure. Consequently, tribal cohesion was minimal, without central leadership, and consisted basically of recognition of a distinct culture, and hospitality towards those of like customs, language and dress. Similarly, members of a particular Apache band had a degree of internal unity, claiming certain hunting grounds, recognising one another's distinctive dialect, and acknowledging the band into which they were born throughout their life. Central leadership and joint political action were, however, very limited and rarely seen.

The largest practical unit was the local group, the nucleus of government, social organisation, hunting, warfare and the practice of religious ceremonies. The hostile environment which prevented a closely knit society at tribal level, conversely encouraged the gregarious nature and cohesion of the Apache people within the local group. This was further enhanced by the close relationships between most members of the local group, either by blood or marriage. They gathered together, around an elder who acted as spokesman, and by whose name the group might be known.

A beautiful example of an Apache war-charm necklace of shell and stone tied into entwined leather thongs, hung with eagle 'fluffies' and feathers. (Arizona State Museum, University of Arizona: photo Helga Teiwes)

Local group leadership was the most extensive example of Apache government and was the position that tribal chiefs such as Cochise and Victorio held. The local group leader was expected to display courage in war, generosity towards the needy, and eloquence in speaking at public occasions. He was also expected to demonstrate an affinity with the Apache's sacred powers, through the knowledge and authority to perform certain religious ceremonies. Like the Plains Indian chiefs, an Apache leader did not dictate to his people, but exerted his influence upon them, promoting decisions he believed to be for the common good. His rôle was to maintain harmony through consultation with other family heads, and to arbitrate in disputes among the Apaches, who had a

An Apache 'flop-head' war-club, clearly showing the rawhide encasement, and a superb horse-hair trailer. (Arizona State Museum, University of Arizona: photo Helen Teiwes)

keen sense of family honour. A popular spokesman who proved to be a good provider would lead a thriving local group, while a declining leader would be gently displaced as another man's voice gained more weight in council. An inadequate man rarely rose to prominence, for the Apaches knew their men too well. While the local group leader's rôle was not hereditary, a leader's son often inherited the status simply through the influence and education which he had gained from his father.

The local group comprised up to 30 extended families. These ideally consisted of a man and wife, unmarried sons and daughters, and married daughters with their husbands and children gathered into a family cluster, each nuclear family occupying a separate dwelling. The local group was associated with a particular settlement, and often known by the name of a nearby landmark such as a river or forest. The settlement, a place of superior defence, shelter, and food, water and grazing resources, provided a focal point for the local group. Family headmen met there to discuss the exploitation of the surrounding resources. The actual execution of most economic tasks was carried out by the extended family, who were reasonably self sufficient within the local group's confines. They would leave the settlement to hunt or gather food and return to process it.

The Apache women provided the constant thread through generations of an extended family, since after marriage it was customary for a man to join his wife's relatives. While marriage often took place between unrelated members of the same local group, if a man did marry into an outside group he had to make the transition to life in another territory.

Women were eligible for marriage after puberty, men after they had accepted adult responsibilities as warriors and hunters, usually in their early twenties. The marriage ceremony was simple, usually involving an exchange of gifts (as in the case of the Plains Indians), which might persist between the intermarried families for several years. The construction of a new shelter for the married couple within the girl's family cluster, confirmed the marriage. The newly married man showed respect for his new relatives through avoidance practices and the use of polite forms of speech. He was obliged to work for his wife's parents, who called him 'h who carries burdens for me'. While the Apache was fiercely individual, he was also taught from an early age to put the good of his extended family first. A conscientious husband could, after becoming the head of his own family, aspire to leadership of the extended family, and eventually of the local group.

While polygamy was reported in all Apache tribes except the Lipan, it was not a common practice. Only a wealthy man might marry twice, and usually to the sister of his first wife.

The division of the Apache tribal groups into bands, local groups and extended families was further complicated in the case of the Western Apache by the existence of a matrilineal clan system reminiscent of the Western Pueblo. There were 62 clans, their members claiming descent from mythological women, and the clans taking their names—e.g. 'two rows of yellow spruce coming together people'—from the farm sites these women established. All clans were ultimately descended from one of three mythological clans, so forming phratries. These clans and phratries interwove all the Western Apache groups. Since a clan's members felt obliged to aid each other, they consequently created extensive tribal links, binding together the isolated local groups. A man's clan could apparently be identified through peculiarities in ceremony, mannerisms, dress—merely by the tilt of his headband—and by clan designs embellishing clothing and possessions.

Marriage between members of clans related to each other within the same phratry was prohibited in the Western Apache, just as the other Apache tribes scorned marriage between close kin. Incest was very closely linked in Apache beliefs to evil witchcraft, the practical necessity of preventing such marriages thus being emphasised through the medium of religion.

Hunting and Gathering

'Apacheria', the land of the Apaches, was a rugged, hostile territory of climatic extremes, descending from forested mountain peaks to desert lowlands, with temperatures ranging from August's 100°F to below zero in winter. Through the evolution of generations, the Apaches developed an innate knowledge of, and affinity with, their homeland. Against a daunting backdrop of canyons, mesas and deserts, they hunted, foraged and fought to survive,

just as the woodrat, lizard and rattlesnake survived.

The Apache eked out a contented, if challenging existence by hunting game and foraging for fruits, seeds and roots of wild plants. A limited amount of agriculture was practised, particularly among the Jicarilla, Western Apache and Lipan, who planted and irrigated plots of corn, beans, maize and squash. All the Apache, however, were primarily hunters and gatherers.

The wild game of Apacheria was as varied as the terrain itself. Deer, antelope, elk and bighorn were the principal large prey in the mountains, foothills and flatlands, while the Mescalero, Jicarilla, Lipan and Kiowa-Apache also ventured on to the Plains in search of buffalo. Diet was supplemented by meat from smaller animals such as woodrats, cottontail rabbits and opossums. Added to this was the Spanish bounty of strayed and captured domestic cattle, as well as horses and mules which were eaten

A fine example of a rawhide medicine-shield, decorated with cloth border, paint designs and hawk feathers, and imparting both physical and supernatural protection to the Apache warrior. (Arizona State Museum, University of Arizona: photo Helga Teiwes)

to stave off starvation. Despite the fact that their lands yielded only enough to survive, and no more, some Apache groups rejected the meat of certain animals in accordance with religious taboos. Coyotes, bears, and snakes were commonly feared as carriers of sickness and embodiments of evil spirits. Certain birds, such as the turkey, were not eaten because of their own diet of worms and insects; while fish, because of their slimy, scaly surface, were associated with the snake.

Hunting was the responsibility of the men, who usually worked alone, in pairs, or in small groups. They chased large game on horseback with lance and bow, used masks crafted from animals' heads to approach deer and antelope on foot, and trapped animals in snares. The men sometimes co-operated in mounted relays to run deer to exhaustion, while the local group might provide the numbers required to surround buffalo, antelope or even rabbits. Among the Chiricahua, however, hunting was so

male-dominated that even the presence of a basket woven by a woman might be considered unlucky.

Apache boys learnt the art of bow and arrow from their grandfathers, and after making their first small kill were taught the whistles, calls, habits, and religious mystique of all the animals and birds. The mature hunter was as keen, cunning and hardy as the animals he sought, and knew the peculiarities of his hunting grounds instinctively. As one old Apache commented: 'There is food everywhere if one only knows how to find it.' This was paralleled in the religion of the Western Apache, who believed that a hunter was less successful in a neighbouring group's territory because he drew power from the very ground itself when hunting in his own lands.

The gathering of vital wild plant harvests for food, medicines and weaving materials was the women's prerogative. They knew their land as intricately as the men, and camps were regularly relocated as the seasons changed and women frantically sought to harvest the numerous different plants as they ripened. Young girls were taught to rise early, and to be strong and vigorous. They were trained to carry wood and keep a fresh supply of water; to flesh, tan, dye and sew buckskin into clothes, bags and parfleches; to weave baskets, and fashion them into water-carriers with a covering of piñon pitch; to dry and store foods; to supervise the home and children, and to prepare the meals. So, too, were they instructed in the vital lore of harvesting and preparing the wild plants.

The Apaches tended to endure the cold of winter in villages on the desert lowlands where the cold was not so extreme. When spring arrived in March the members of a local group travelled back into the mountains to their main settlement. Here they established their clusters of 'wickiups': domed shelters consisting of cottonwood poles set in a circular trench, bent and lashed together at the top with yucca fibre. Except in times of wind and rain this framework was only partially covered, with a thatch of bear grass tied with yucca fronds and usually with several hides. While the wickiup was

An Apache baby bound into a typical cradleboard of wicker and cloth, with several protective amulets on a large sun shade, and decoration of a distinctive T-shaped beaded ornament, and beaded drops. Early 1900s. Around it are baskets, pitch-covered water jar, burden basket, bow and arrow and cloth saddlebag. (Arizona State Museum, University of Arizona)

A traditional Western Apache buckskin blouse decorated with beadwork and tin cone pendants. (Arizona State Museum, University of Arizona: photo Helga Teiwes)

he typical Apache dwelling, being easily con-
tructed and as easily abandoned in flight from an
nemy, the tipi was often erected on the flatlands,
articularly by those tribes showing most Plains
nfluence.

Digging sticks broke the ground for the planting
f crops, perhaps watered by irrigation ditches. The
rops were tended by the young and elderly, while
here was a constant coming and going of hunting
nd gathering parties. The women of the extended
amily formed a stable, experienced gathering unit,
ften departing to a nearby gathering ground for a
ay's work. Major expeditions were also organised,
onsisting of large hunting parties, gathering
roups, or a combination of the two, leaving the
ettlement for weeks at a time.

After the welcome gathering of the first green
egetables, the narrow-leafed yucca, parties of
omen sought out the yucca flowers, arrowheads,
ild onions, cacti fruits and various berries of spring
nd early summer. The largest expedition took
lace in May, when the majority of the local group's
omen, with all the male assistance they could
uster, travelled to an area abundant in the new,
owering, reddish spike-leaved stalks of the mescal

or agave, also known as the century plant. The
mescal stalks were cut, pounded and roasted, and
the heavy, fleshy tubers or crowns were prised from
the ground with hammers and pointed sticks.

The women worked feverishly, gathering great
quantities of the two-foot-diameter mescal crowns
and loading them into a huge roasting pit hacked
out of the hard, dry soil. Hot stones steamed the
mescal into a paste, which was eaten immediately or
pounded into flat cakes and sun-dried. The dried
mescal was carried home by heavily laden horses,
strung out in pack trains, accompanied by the
singing, chattering women. The mescal was highly
nutritious and could be preserved indefinitely,
providing an important staple of the Apache diet.

Throughout the summer and autumn plants
were gathered: wild potatoes, and a mixture of
acorns, hackberries and mesquite beans, made into
crude breads; chokecherries and raspberries dried
into cakes; sumal and juniper berries, strawberries,
grapes and sweet pink yucca fruit; and wild
tobacco, which was cut and cured. In the evenings

the extended family's women prepared meals from their spoils and meat, often under shades called ramadas or 'squaw-coolers'.

In October the domestic corn was harvested, and eaten, preserved or brewed by the women into a weak corn beer, called 'tiswin' by the whites. Late autumn provided the best hunting, while women and children amassed copious quantities of acorns, piñon nuts and seeds. As winter, the season called Ghost Face, approached, the Apaches sought the shelter of lowland villages. Gathering largely ceased, while raiding, preserved foods, a limited amount of small game, and food taken in emergencies from secret caches in sealed caves fed the Apache until the yucca stalks reannounced the arrival of spring.

The Apaches were supremely dependent upon nature. Tribal variations on the seasonal pattern varied simply with environment, as each band exploited whatever its particular area yielded.

A 1911 photograph of an Apache woman carrying her child in woven burden basket by means of a headstrap. She wears traditional fringed buckskin blouse decorated with pain beadwork, tin cone pendants, and brass studs. (Arizona Stat Museum, University of Arizona)

War

The Apache drew a sharp distinction between warfare and raiding. Their respective aims were summarised by the Western Apache words for each: raiding was 'to search out enemy property', while war meant 'to take death from an enemy'.

The raid was prompted by the announcement, usually from an older woman, that the meat supply was approaching exhaustion. The local group's leader, or an experienced warrior, would shortly thereafter announce plans for an expedition, and call for followers. Usually a raiding party consisted of less than a dozen raiders, for concealment was a prime consideration. The rituals preceding a raid were designed to prevent the raiders' discovery, rather than to fortify them for war.

In early times the raids were directed against other Indian tribes, such as the Comanches, but latterly the Spanish and Mexicans generously, if unwittingly, supplied horses and other livestock to the clandestine raiders. Having reached enemy territory the Apache raiders proceeded with great stealth, until they located a tribe's herd. Then, in the early hours of morning, two or three men silently coaxed the livestock a safe distance from the

camp, where their fellow raiders encircled them an drove them off. The return journey was made a rapidly as possible, and by travelling without slee for up to five days the Apache raiders usually mad a successful escape. They avoided fighting, for th would alert their enemies for miles around an defeat the purpose of the raid. If they were pursue and caught the raiders preferred to kill the capture animals, scatter, and return later to devour thei spoils.

Upon returning to camp the raiders distribute the livestock among their relatives. They were als obliged to present a proportion of their spoils t widows and divorcées, whose request was embodie in singing and dancing. This ensured an eve distribution of meat throughout the local group.

War parties were organised to avenge the death of Apache raiders, or Apache families killed b other tribes' raiding parties. The deceased relatives initiated the organisation of the war part They called for warriors—particularly kinsmen o the slain Apache—from other local groups to mee at an arranged rendezvous. Here a war ceremon was conducted, called 'stiff hide spread on th round' by the Western Apache. A shaman versed in the supernatural songs and ceremonials of war conducted prayers exhorting success for, and blood lust in, the warriors, who sang softly and joined the dancing to signify their participation in the war party.

War parties might contain as many as 200 men. Among them would be at least one shaman, who conducted prayers exhorting success for, and blood the venture before they departed. He continued to conduct his ceremonies on the warpath, while also encouraging respectful behaviour from the warriors, for war was a religious undertaking. Having ensured the safety of their local group camps, who might scatter and reunite at a new campsite to avoid back-tracking, the war party departed. They travelled warily, posting scouts when they camped (usually on the highest possible terrain, no matter how far from water and wood), until they reached their target. They often made their attack from several directions at once.

The Apaches preferred to make a surprise attack shortly before dawn. Only the Lipan and the Kiowa-Apache counted coup, the other Apaches extracting revenge by killing as many of the enemy as possible. Scalping was rare, and was probably only practised against the Mexicans in retaliation for their own outrages. (The taking of scalps was not consistent with Apache fears of contamination from the dead, and if practised by a Jicarilla, for example, it required lengthy ritual preparation and subsequent purification.) A single significant victory was usually sufficient to persuade the warriors to return home, particularly if they had acquired livestock and other booty. They were welcomed with celebratory feasting and dancing.

The Apaches were trained for war from boyhood. Boys woke early and bathed in the river, even if they had to crack the surface ice to do so. They ran up hillsides and back with a mouthful of water, to learn correct breathing through the nose, and the endurance so characteristic of the Apaches. Boys were hardened by rough wrestling games and mock battles, and taught by their relatives the geography, attributes and sanctity of their surroundings.

When he felt ready, an Apache youth began the novice warrior complex of his first four raids, which were permeated with religious beliefs and ritual. Having been accepted as a member of his first

raiding party the adolescent was usually instructed by a war shaman, who gave him a drinking tube and scratcher embellished with lightning designs, and a special war cap which, unlike those of the mature warriors, did not bestow spiritual 'power'. Among the Western Apache the men and women of the camp formed a line, and blessed the boy with pollen as he departed.

A White Mountain Apache male doll of cloth, buckskin, feathers, beads and horsehair. (Arizona State Museum, University of Arizona: photo Helga Teiwes)

During the expedition the apprentice warrior was considered sacred, being identified with the culture-hero called Child of the Water. He was obliged to use the ceremonial warpath language, using ritual phrases to replace words for common objects during the raid. He used the scratcher to scratch himself and the drinking tube to ensure water did not touch his lips. The boy also observed such taboos as only eating food after it had grown cold, to bring the raiders good fortune.

The novice's practical rôle was subservient to the other warriors. He fetched wood and water, cooked the food, and guarded the camp at night. If he followed his instructions well, he would be allowed to accompany the warriors on a subsequent raid. If he completed the sacred number of four raids without deviations in his conduct, the novice received the coveted reward of recognition as an Apache warrior.

The legendary skill and endurance of the Apache warriors is supported by the testimonies of the white soldiers who fought them. The 'tigers of the human race', as Gen. George Crook described the Apaches, were ideally adapted to fighting in their rugged homeland. A warrior usually wore a shirt, a breechclout, and moccasins, often reaching above the knee; he carried a rope, blanket, water jar, fire drill, rations of mescal or jerky, and his weapons. He might employ a shield, bow and arrows, lance, war club, knife and, particularly during the Apache Wars, a gun and cartridge belts. The Apaches often

blackened their weapons for camouflage (which explains the Mexican name for Warm Spring leader Cuchillo Negro, 'Black Knife').

An Apache could live instinctively off the land and when nature was ungenerous he could withstand extraordinary extremes of thirst and hunger. A warrior's only other requirements were the amulets prepared by a shaman possessing the ceremonials of war. Buckskin cords and string worn around the head and over the shoulder; war shirts; medicine shields; tight-fitting war caps adorned with owl and turkey feathers, and numerous other ornaments were embellished with designs invoking the protection and potency of the sacred powers and their bird and animal messengers. Paint was daubed across the warrior's face to invoke the particular power of a war shaman, and bags of sacred cattail pollen or '*hoddentin*' were carried to make morning and evening offerings.

The possession of supernatural 'enemies-against' power was a prized gift, and could be gained either from communion with the sacred powers or directly from a war shaman who had so acquired it. The ceremonials invoking such power might be directed toward protecting a warrior, concealing a war

White Mountain Apache infant's moccasins, decorated with tin cone pendants. (Arizona State Museum, University of Arizona: photo Helga Teiwes)

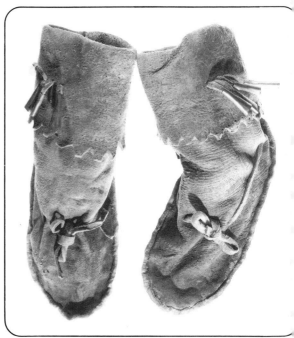

Traditional Western Apache beaded moccasins, with buckskin uppers and rawhide soles. (Arizona State Museum, University of Arizona: photo Helga Teiwes)

arty, bestowing speed of running, or locating an
nemy. Geronimo was a war shaman whose power
llegedly enabled him to predict events, and
revented his being killed by bullets. Victorio's
ster, Lozen, who was a woman warrior—a rare
hing indeed—had great power: stretching out her
rms and praying, she was supposed to be able to
etermine the proximity of an enemy by the
ntensity of the tingling in her palms.

While the Apache did adopt a horse culture
ased on that of the Spaniards, their terrain and
festyle did not lend itself to the adoption of the
orse in the same way as did that of the Plains
ndians. Horses were often used during large raids,
ut a warrior was equally likely to travel on foot,
llowing him to use the concealment offered by his
errain. The broad-chested, sinewy Apache warrior
uld run as much as 70 miles a day, and his
mooth, effortless stride' was such that, to Lt.
ritton Davis, 'the thought of attempting to catch
ne of them in the mountains gave me a queer
eling of helplessness'. The women were also
xtraordinary runners, and thought nothing of
otting 60 miles to present candy to their children
hen they had been placed in boarding schools in
ter years.

The Apache's adeptness at concealment was
emonstrated to Capt. John C. Cremony by the
Mescalero called Quick Killer. On an open plain,
Quick Killer told Cremony to turn his back, and in
n instant had disappeared. Failing to find him,
remony called for Quick Killer to reveal himself,
hereupon the much amused Apache emerged
om the spot a few feet away where he had
ompletely buried himself under thick grama grass.
The warriors' skills were easily adapted to the
uerrilla war they fought against the Spaniards,
Mexicans and Americans. Few pursuers success-
lly found their way into the labyrinthine
rongholds of Apacheria until they learned to turn
pache against Apache, harnessing the remarkable
acking abilities of the scouts. If chased closely an
pache group would scatter, running across rocks
an agreed rendezvous, and leaving no trail.
umerous secret supply caches fed the group, who
sited at night the waterholes which they knew well
could quickly spot from high ground. If pressed
rd they might kill their horses and climb 'like
er' up seemingly impassable cliffsides.

A young Apache woman photographed in 1920. She wears a
typical cluster of bead necklaces, and her cape appears to be
tied both at the neck and around the waist. (Arizona State
Museum, University of Arizona: photo Forman Hanna)

False camps were sometimes pitched, and
livestock driven several miles ahead of the actual
area where a group concealed themselves. Camps
could be moved silently, and were at times moved
right under the noses of the Apaches' enemies.
Adept at flight, the Apaches were also skilled in
doubling back 'like a fox' and ambushing their
pursuers.

The Apaches, in contrast to the Plains Indians,
applauded courage but derided heroics: their
numbers were too few for flamboyant risks and
needless loss of life. Stealth and caution were
encouraged—though when the Apache was wounded or cornered there was no more ferocious
adversary.

15

Religion

The Apaches had a rich cycle of sacred myths to explain the origins of their ceremonies and religious beliefs. An unclearly defined Supreme Being was referred to as *Usen* or Life Giver; and myths among the Jicarilla, Lipan and Western Apache told of their people's emergence from within the earth. The popular mythological trickster figure of Coyote created daylight through playing a 'moccasin game', pitting creatures of the night against the victorious creatures of the day. Since the contest resulted in daybreak, whenever the Apache played the moccasin game they would blacken their faces if ever it continued beyond sunrise. Coyote exemplified the virtues and failings of man, securing such necessities as fire while simultaneously demonstrating the vices—gluttony, falsehood, incest—of which the Apaches strongly disapproved.

The most prominent Apache supernaturals were the sacred maiden White Painted Woman (White Shell Woman, Changing Woman) and her son Child of the Water. His brother, Killer of Enemies is also prominent, though at times the two seem synonymous. Myths of the Apache's early existence focus on White Painted Woman's divine conception of her sons, and their slaying of the evil monster that inhabited the Earth. The mythological exploit of the culture-heroes, and the rituals and object they employed, were adopted by the Apaches into their ceremonies. The central participants in the girl's puberty rite and the boy's novice raiding complex were identified with White Painted Woman and Child of the Water respectively.

The Apaches believed the Universe to be permeated with supernatural power, which could be sought by man through prayer, or through a long period of isolated instruction from a shaman who possessed power. Those people who were themselves sought out by a power were regarded as particularly worthy and sacred. A power appeared to its recipient through visionary experience in the form of an animal, bird or natural force related to its type. The visionary was often led to a holy home such as a mountain cave, where he received the

Gan or Mountain Spirit dancers, early 1900s, probably Western Apache judging by the elaborate fan-racks. They wear blankets instead of buckskin kilts, and the central figure wears boots rather than moccasins. However, their extensive black and white body paint, and their wands, cloth and eagle feather arm-trailers, bandanas, masks with false button eyes, and racks clearly bearing snake designs, are traditional. Note the sacred clown on the left wearing a mask, small rack, arm trailers and white, black-speckled paint. They form the old time *gan* group of four dancers, symbolising the Four Directions, complemented by a clown. (Arizona State Museum, University of Arizona: photo Forman Hanna)

songs, prayers and ceremonies which were part of, and belonged to, the power; and with which it could be manipulated by the visionary.

Under the guidance of an established shaman a visionary learnt the extent of his power, and its accompanying taboos, for the supernatural had to be treated with great respect. Because illness was so catastrophic to people of a hunting and gathering economy, most powers and their rituals were curative; others were used for such purposes as protection on the warpath, and even to attain success in gambling. Female shamans were apparently quite common, while the possession of power was considered vital to a man who aspired to leadership.

Power could also be used for evil, however. The Apache had strong witchcraft fears, believing witches to covertly cause sickness and even death through the misuse of their powers. Those tried and found guilty of witchcraft—in a trial the Western Apache termed 'they are talking about witches'—were at the very least expelled from the local group.

Closely associated with such witchcraft fears was the distress caused by the presence of creatures such as owls, coyotes, bears and snakes. Such evil familiars were believed to contain the ghosts of witches and other restless spirits who had not departed peacefully after death to the Apaches' parallel underworld. On one of Crook's expeditions into the Sierra Madre his Apache scouts suddenly halted, refusing to go any further until the photographer A. Frank Randall released the owl he had caught and tied to his saddle. Shamans who had power over such creatures, and who could cure the sicknesses they caused, were afforded great respect.

The most noted traditional Apache ceremony was the girl's puberty rite. As a child grew up, various rituals were conducted in prayer for a long and healthy life. Amulets were ritually hung on a baby's cradle board to protect the child, who was particularly vulnerable to evil. When able to walk, the child was led in new footwear along a trail of pollen leading east, in the 'putting on moccasins' ceremony. In the haircutting rite the following spring—a time of new growth—the child's hair was cut, with a few tufts left to encourage healthy growth of new hair and, by extension, of the child. At puberty it was hoped that a boy would make his

A striking 1890s portrait of an unidentified Apache scout wearing a breech-clout over a thin leather belt. The holster on his cartridge-belt holds a US Army Colt revolver. (Arizona State Museum, University of Arizona)

first four sacred raids, while a girl performed the puberty rite, also called the Sunrise Dance.

In the four-day puberty rite, the girl was considered sacred, being identified with White Painted Woman. She wore a beautifully decorated dress of the finest buckskin, coloured yellow to symbolise the sacred pollen. She carried a scratching stick and drinking tube, a cane to symbolise longevity, and wore symbols such as eagle feathers, and shell ornaments which represented White Painted Woman. The ceremonies began on the first morning when the girl, her face daubed with pollen, was led to the ceremonial tipi by the specially appointed shaman whose relentless chanting of songs and prayers accompanied the rituals. The girl knelt on a buckskin, her hands raised to the

un, in the mythological position assumed by White Painted Woman. Then she lay prone and her female sponsor, a woman of exemplary reputation, massaged her, ensuring her strength as an adult. The sponsor then pushed the girl away, and she ran to the four directions, circling a basket laden with ritual objects, and so receiving a blessing of quickness.

In the evening the maiden attended the ritual singing and dancing in the ceremonial tipi, while social dancing took place outside. Then came the appearance of one of the most dramatic features pervading the ceremonies of the Apache tribes: the masked impersonators of the Mountain Spirits who protected the tribes. The '*gan*' or Mountain Spirit dancers invoked the power of these supernaturals to cure illness, drive away evil and bring good fortune. They assembled in a cave in the mountains, and under the guidance of a *gan* shaman donned their sacred regalia. As impersonators of the supernatural they manipulated great power, and therefore observed severe restrictions. To don the *gan* mask without correct ritual; to recognise a friend beneath the mask; to dance incorrectly or to tamper with *gan* regalia after it had been ritually abandoned in a secret cache, might cause sickness, madness or death.

At the appropriate moment in the puberty rite the gan dancers descended from their mountain hideaway. They wore buckskin moccasins and skirts, and masks of black buckskin topped with towering, decorated horns of yucca. Their bodies bore striking paint designs of lightning and other sacred symbols, and they were adorned with red flannel and eagle feather streamers, turquoise and abalone.

Emerging from the darkness four times, they danced, stamped and threatened around a blazing fire, brandishing and thrusting great decorated wands. The *gan*—their groups of four each accompanied by the antics of a white, black-spotted

An Apache warrior's buckskin war-medicine cap, adorned with brass tacks, a silver conch, and eagle feathers. (Arizona State Museum, University of Arizona: photo Helga Teiwes)

clown, a contrary figure of humour and sanctity—were powerful healers and great entertainers.

On the fourth night the ceremonies continued until dawn, when the puberty rite shaman painted on his palm a sun symbol which he pressed to the girl's head as the sun rose. She then performed another four ritual circles, the ceremonial tipi being dismantled as she ran. The hiring of the various skilled ceremonialists (who might be masters of up to 80 complex chants), the feeding of the spectators, and the dressing of the maiden represented an expensive undertaking for the girl's family; but the puberty rite was considered a vital, sacred confirmation of the beginning of womanhood.

The Jicarilla termed their traditional rituals 'long life' ceremonies, which, aside from the puberty rite, included the curative Holiness Rite and the Ceremonial Relay. The Holiness Rite, which featured the most arduous shamanic rôle, the impersonation of the Bear and Snake, the obscene performance of black- and brown-striped clowns, and the depositing of sickness on a ritually prepared tree, was performed to cure the powerful Snake and Bear sicknesses.

The Relay Race was representative of the dual food supply, and featured the sacred sand paintings used also by the Western Apache and Navajo. Ritually painted runners from the Ollero band, representing Sun and the animals, raced the Llanero athletes, who symbolised Moon and the

Qua-tha-hooly-hooly or Quatha-hooa-hooba (Yellow Face), a scout, photographed in a studio, probably in 1886. While his costume could easily be that of an Apache scout, he is in fact identified as a Mojave, sometimes called Apache-Mojave, and thus belongs to the Yuman linguistic group of the South-West. He wears a cartridge belt and holds a US Army revolver. Note the large awl-case, decorated with tin cone pendants and beadwork, hanging from the left side of his belt: such cases were popular among the Apaches. (Arizona State Museum, University of Arizona) plants. If the Olleros won, game would be abundant that year, while a Llanero victory symbolised success in gathering plants. Such ceremonies, stemming from myths and integrated into Apache culture, were profuse before the intervention of the white man.

The Apache Wars

The Spaniards

Drawn by the prospect of converts to the Roman Catholic faith and by the legends of mineral riches, the Spanish conquistadores inevitably ventured beyond their northern frontier in Mexico into the lands of the Apaches. When Francisco Vasquez de Coronado's expedition plundered the pueblos of the Rio Grande in 1540 the Apaches were well established in their traditional homeland in the South-West, although the eastern Apaches were divided into poorly defined bands on the borders of the Plains. Various subsequent expeditions continued to advertise the brutality of Spanish colonialism, and set the pattern of Spanish soldiers raiding to acquire Indian slaves, under the guise of extending the boundaries of civilisation. The

capture of Indians for sale in the thriving slave market obviously did nothing to enrich relations between Apache and Spaniard.

In 1598 Juan de Onate, the first Spanish governor of New Mexico, founded a colony in the Rio Grande valley. In 1599 his soldiers attacked the Acoma Pueblo of the Keres, killing 800 and capturing nearly 600; whereupon he barbarously sentenced captured males over the age of 25 to have one foot cut off and to serve 20 years of slavery. It seems likely that Apaches, allies of the Keres, were present in the defence of Acoma. Certainly, in the years that followed, Apache or Navajo raided Onate's first capital at San Gabriel with such ferocity that it was moved to Santa Fé in 1610. By 1630 the Apaches were using horses both for mount and food, and a familiar pattern of conflict with the Spaniards had developed. When Apaches came to trade with the Pueblo Indians, the Spanish trapped them and sold them into slavery. The Apache consequently nurtured a burning hatred for the Spanish and Mexicans, and retaliated with raids destructive and frequent enough to cause the abandonment of many settlements. While the sedentary Pueblos faced confiscation of crops or annihilation by superior arms if they challenged Spanish supremacy, the elusively mobile Apache could strike viciously and recoil swiftly, using their ancient skills to evade pursuit.

To a degree, the Spanish invasion altered the Apaches' subsistence practices. Larger raiding parties were required, and families could no longer be left undefended; so, raiding became a constant practice for the whole local group, and stolen livestock compensated, to a certain extent, for the disrupted gathering of plants. Raiders frequently refrained from destroying settlements outright while they remained they were a valuable economic resource—the Spaniards produced livestock and grain, which the Apache raiders duly collected.

Apache ambushes and raids were frequent from 1660 to 1680, when the Pueblo Revolt, abetted by some Apache groups, drove the Spanish from New Mexico. Despite the Spanish reconquest 12 years

Apache rawhide playing cards, derived from Spanish model showing the typical deck of four ten-card suits: clockwise from bottom left, the suits are clubs, coins, cups and swords. Each suit runs from ace to seven, with picture cards representing page, mounted knight and king, in designs of red, yellow and black paint. (Arizona State Museum, University of Arizona, photo Helga Teiwes)

Western Apache 'Pinal-Coyotero' delegation, San Carlos Reservation, Arizona, before 1877: *left to right*: **Napasgingush, wife of Eskinilay, Cullah, Eskinilay, Passalah, Pinal and son, Hautsuhnehay, Eskayelah, Skellegunney, and Cushshashado. (Arizona State Museum, University of Arizona)**

ater, and the establishment of presidios along the northern frontier, the Apaches continued to raid deep into Mexico and Texas. By 1700 each tribe was firmly established in its traditional territory, and the pattern of raids and Spanish punitive expeditions continued throughout the 18th century. The Spanish used auxiliaries from tribes such as the Opata to bolster their defences. After 1714 Jicarilla Apaches were also used as auxiliaries, and were part of the force which defeated the Comanche in 1779.

After 1786 the Spanish departed from their impotent policy of extermination against the Apaches, when Viceroy Bernardo de Gálvez introduced a new approach. Tribes were to be encouraged to wage war against one another; and those seeking peace were to be settled on reservations—'establecimiento de paz'—near the Spanish presidios, and supplied with rations and inferior Spanish firearms to make them dependent upon the Spaniards. Gálvez also recommended supplying the Apaches with alcohol, as '. . . a means of gaining their goodwill, discovering their secrets, calming them so they will think less often of conceiving and executing their hostilities, and creating for them a new necessity which will oblige them to recognise their dependence upon us more directly'.

The new policy enjoyed moderate success, leading to a period of relative calm from 1790 to 1830. Chiricahua groups settled near Bacoachi in 1786 (although their most friendly chief, Isosé, was killed by hostile Chiricahuas in 1788). Peaceful Indians joined the Spaniards in pursuing the hostiles, illustrating Spanish success in breaking tribal strength. Similarly, the alliance between Apache and Navajo was ruptured after Gileños killed the Navajo chief Antonio El Pinto for helping the Spanish against them. By 1793 eight reservations contained as many as 2,000 Apaches, and in 1810 the Mescalero were granted land rights and rations.

The Mexicans

After the declaration of Mexican Independence the Apache situation deteriorated. The Mexican government could not afford to man the presidios efficiently, and their lack of funds reduced subsidies for the system of supplying rations to the Apaches, undermining any treaties between the Apaches and the Mexicans. Raiding was resumed with great ferocity in the 1830s, depopulating much of poorly defended northern Sonora and Chihuahua.

The deeply-ingrained Apache hatred of the Mexicans was intensified when, in 1825, the governor of Sonora offered a bounty of 100 pesc ($100) for the scalp of any Apache warrior ove fourteen. This bounty was imitated by Chihuahu province in 1837, and was even extended to 50 pesc for women's scalps and 25 pesos for those c children.

In 1822 the Mexicans had resumed working th copper mines at Santa Rita, under the protection c Juan José Compá, leader of the Coppermin Mimbreños. In 1837 Juan José was invited by a American trader called James Johnson, whom h believed to be a trusted friend, to attend a feast. Th chief complied; but as his people ate and drank Johnson fired a hail of grapeshot from a conceale howitzer into their midst, and his armed associate then completed the bloody massacre. Juan José

A 1981 Apache Puberty Rite on the San Carlos Reservation Watched by her sponsor, and accompanied by the beating drums, the maiden seeks the blessing of the sun; a piece of abalone shell in her hair symbolising her rôle as White Shell Woman. (Arizona State Museum, University of Arizona)

calp was among the many that Johnson and his ellow bounty hunters subsequently carried to onora to exchange for their blood money.

Juan José's successor was Mangas Coloradas— ed Sleeves—a huge man with a mane of black air, renowned as a warrior and statesman. He ented his fury against the Mexican settlers at Santa ita by waylaying the 'conducta' which supplied em with provisions. As the settlers were forced to bandon the safety of the fort they were killed by the Iimbreño warriors. The territory of the Iimbreños remained unsafe after the abandon- ent of Santa Rita, the scalp bounties naturally elling the bitter conflict between the Apaches and e Mexicans.

War with the Americans

fter the signing of the Treaty of Guadalupe idalgo of 1848, ceding the Spanish South-West d its Indian tribes to the United States, American oops were withdrawn from Mexico. Despite the nited States' agreement to stop the Apaches ossing the new border, the raids upon which the ibes had grown to depend continued. The paches failed to understand the Americans' titude towards raiding into Mexico.

Cochise and Mangas Coloradas

In the aftermath of the 1851 Boundaries Commission, miners reopened the Santa Rita coppermines and discovered gold at nearby Pinos Altos. Mangas Coloradas reputedly visited the miners' camp and offered to lead them to greater gold deposits. Fearing a trap, they bound the great chief to a tree and whipped him brutally. His rage made him an implacable enemy of the Americans in the years to come. After the 1853 Gadsen Purchase Apache distrust grew and spread, as an increasing number of American settlers entered their lands. The attention of the Americans was focused on the Chiricahuas who, although friendly enough to safeguard the passage of the Butterfield Stage, provided the main obstacle to American settlement of New Mexico.

In January 1861 Lt. George Bascom of the 7th Infantry led 54 mounted infantrymen to Apache Pass, seeking the return of two kidnapped boys. Cochise, the great leader of the Central Chiricahua, was asked to come to Bascom's tent, and arrived at the head of a small group. He suggested that the boys had been kidnapped by Coyotero Apaches, and offered to intervene. Bascom wrongly accused Cochise of the crime, however, insisting that he would be held prisoner until the boys were returned. Alarmed and angry, the chief instantly drew a knife, slashed the tent, and escaped the soldiers who had gathered around him; but the other Chiricahuas were held as hostages. Cochise returned with his own hostages—captured Butterfield Mail employees—and offered to exchange them for his own people. In an atmosphere of mutual distrust, Cochise's followers and Bascom's troops became involved in a brief skirmish, and both men killed their hostages.

In the years that followed, the US troops were withdrawn from the Apache's lands to fight the Civil War. Cochise took this opportunity, assisted by Mangas Coloradas, to drive the settlers away by relentless raiding. Treaties were abandoned, and once again an extermination policy was adopted against the Apaches. In 1862 Gen. James Carleton's California Volunteers repossessed New Mexico and Arizona from the Confederates. A despatch unit under Capt. Roberts was sent through Apache Pass, where Cochise and Mangas Coloradas lay in wait.

Scouts, possibly Yuman, with US Army officers. The uniformed scout, Na-da-sa, wears a Mills cartridge-belt and holds a Springfield rifle. (Arizona State Museum, University of Arizona)

The artillery accompanying the soldiers defeated the ambush, however, and Mangas Coloradas was shot from his horse. He was carried to Janos, where doctors were told to cure him or their town would be destroyed. He survived; but a year later ventured, under a flag of truce, into the camp of Capt. Shirland's California Volunteers, to parley for peace with the miners and soldiers. He was seized as a prisoner, and Gen. West reputedly told his guards: 'I want him dead or alive tomorrow morning do you understand? I want him dead'. The guards were seen during the night heating their bayonets and placing them on the ageing chief's legs; when he remonstrated, they shot him. To complete their work they decapitated him, and boiled his head in a large, black pot. The official report explained that Mangas Coloradas was killed 'while attempting to escape'. Cochise fought on with such warriors as Nana and Victorio of the Warm Springs Apaches by his side.

Carleton's campaigns, in which 'the Indians are to be soundly whipped', were also aimed at the Mescalero and Navajo; and his inflexible policy resulted in the massacre of Manuelito's peaceful Mescalero band in 1862. The two tribes were rounded up and concentrated at the Bosque

Apache Gan Dancers:
1: Western Apache
2: Mescalero Apache
3: Chiricahua Apache

Chiricahua Apache:
1, 2, 4, 6: Warriors
3, 5: Women

Chiricahua Puberty Ceremony:
1: Maiden
2: Sponsor
3: Shaman

C

Western Apache:
1,2: San Carlos warriors
3: Tonto warrior
4: Western Apache fiddle player

5, 8: Western Apache women
6: Western Apache shaman
7: White Mountain woman

D

Mescalero Apache:
1, 2: Warriors
3: Woman

E

Jicarilla Apache:
1, 2: Warriors
3: Woman

F

Apache Scouts:
1, 2, 4: Scouts
3: 1st Sgt. of Scouts

G

Redondo Reservation, despite its unsuitability and their mutual hostility. By 1865 some 9,000 Navajo and 500 Mescaleros were concentrated there in appalling conditions; and the Mescaleros began to slip back to their old lands as Carleton sought unsuccessfully to imprison even more tribes on the reservation. In 1868 the Navajos were permitted to make the joyous 'Long Walk' back to their own country.

Crook's First Campaign

In 1870 President Grant's 'peace policy' provided an alternative to extermination, and was given added impetus by the 1871 Camp Grant Massacre. Peaceful Arivaipa Apache women and children under Eskiminzin were massacred by Tucson citizens and Papago Indians, and the outrages committed created a national outcry. Gen. George Crook was appointed commander of the Depart-

ment of Arizona, to put an end to the fumblings of military and civilian authorities and to enforce settlement of the Apaches on reservations. A peace commission under Vincent Colyer and Gen. Oliver Howard was meanwhile sent to establish the reservations.

Reservations were established at Fort Apache for the Cibecue and northern White Mountain; at Camp Verde for the northern and southern Tonto; and at Camp Grant for the San Carlos and southern White Mountain divisions of the Western Apache tribe. Outbreaks and raids continued, however; and in 1872 Crook embarked on his Tonto Basin campaign. He used the tactics which were to prove so successful in subduing the Apaches, most

Western Apache 'Coyotero' warriors, including the chief Al-che-say, armed with Springfield and Winchester carbines. Note the feathered buckskin war-caps. (**Arizona State Museum, University of Arizona**)

An impressive photograph of US and Apache scouts, under Lt. Maus, 1886, showing variations in scout costumes. (Arizona State Museum, University of Arizona)

particularly by using Apache scouts to harass the hostiles tirelessly, and to demonstrate that they had no place to hide. It became a popular saying that only an Apache could catch an Apache, and Crook once commented: 'To polish a diamond, there is nothing like its own dust'. Part of the reason for Crook's success with his scouts, and in all his dealings with the Apaches, was that they trusted him. He told them the truth, and honesty was a very important virtue among the Apaches.

The most dramatic battle fought against the Tontos was that at Salt River Cave in December 1872. Maj. Brown's column trapped the Apaches in a huge, shallow cave 400 to 500 feet from the top of a cliff. It was seemingly unassailable, being protected by a natural rampart; and the Tontos slapped their buttocks and jeered derisively when asked to surrender. By firing at the cave roof, however, the soldiers ricocheted their bullets down on to the Tonto families. Suddenly, a high-pitched, despairing, yet threatening wail filled the air, which the scouts identified as the death song, meaning that the Apaches were about to charge. The charge was repelled by the soldiers' rapid-fire musketry, and the Apaches were beaten. A similar victory on Turret Mountain secured the surrender of the majority of the Tontos. Crook put a price on the head of the most irreconcilable warrior, Delshay,

An 1885 studio shot of White Mountain Apache Scouts: *left to right:* Das-Luca, Skro-Kit, and Shus-El-Day. They are a magnificent example of the variety seen among Apache scouts' uniforms. All carry Springfield carbines. (Arizona State Museum, University of Arizona)

and two scouts submitted separate heads. 'Being satisfied that both parties were earnest in their beliefs, and the bringing in of an extra head as not amiss, I paid both parties', Crook explained.

By 1870 many Eastern Chiricahuas, including Loco and Victorio, had gathered at Cañada Alamosa Agency near Ojo Caliente (Warm Springs), weary of war. When ordered to move to the Tualarosa Reservation, however, they fled into the mountains. In 1872 Gen. Howard and Thomas Jeffords (a friend of Cochise's since he ventured alone into the Chiricahua stronghold) established a reservation for Cochise's people around the Chiricahua Mountains. It was troubled by visits from Chiricahuas and White Mountain Apaches unhappily situated at Tualarosa and San Carlos, and by its close proximity to the border. Cochise's death in 1874 coincided with requests for the Chiricahua to move to Warm Springs, following the failure of the Cañada Alamosa Agency.

The work of settling the Indians peacefully on reservations was largely undone by the 'concentration' policy implemented after 1875. By virtue of the Indians' love for their own lands, and the enmity between many tribes, a concentration policy inevitably provoked trouble. In February 1875 over 1,400 Tontos and Yavapais made a terrible mountain journey to San Carlos; Levi Edwin Dudley, who supervised the removal, snapped: 'They are Indians—let the beggars walk'. They were joined there by the White Mountain band from Fort Apache in July.

Clum and Victorio

The San Carlos Reservation was run by John P. Clum, whose independent actions, aided by his Apache police, created great conflict with the military. In 1876 Clum arrived to escort the 1,000 Chiricahuas from the Chiricahua Reservation to San Carlos, though many—including the most prominent hostiles Geronimo, Juh (Whoa) and Nolgee—had fled. They took refuge at the Warm Springs Reservation; but in 1877 Clum and his Indian police arrived there and, despite the late arrival of their military back-up, captured Geronimo and escorted the Chiricahuas to San Carlos.

Feeling that his authority was being usurped by the military, Clum resigned in July 1877; and in

Studio shot of an Apache Scout, labelled 'Apache Scout Mike'. He wears distinctive jewellery and face-paint, and holds a Springfield rifle. (Arizona State Museum, University of Arizona)

September, 300 Chiricahuas fled behind Victorio and Loco. Eleven days later 187 of them, including Victorio, surrendered at Fort Wingate, and were taken to Warm Springs, where more hostiles gradually convened. In mid-October 1878, they learned that they were to be escorted back to San Carlos, and Victorio and 80 followers scattered into the hills. In February 1879 Victorio surrendered at Mescalero; but in July, fearing arrest, he fled once again, this time to Mexico. A series of bloody raids followed, and Victorio evaded all attempts at pursuit. Eventually, on 15 October 1880, he died along with most of his warriors in a long battle with Mexican troops. Ironically, just before his flight it had been virtually decided to give the Chiricahua the Warm Springs Reservation which Victorio desired; but his raids caused the suspension of the idea. Victorio's war was continued by the ageing war leader and shaman Nana, whose 40 raiders won eight pitched battles and eluded 1,400 troops during two months of raiding in the summer of 1881, covering 1,000 miles before escaping into Mexico.

In 1881 many despairing San Carlos Indians had turned to the religion of a White Mountain shaman called Nocadelklinny, whose beliefs were reminiscent of the Plains Indian Ghost Dance. Against a backdrop of reservation boredom in the sterile, humid, disease-ridden atmosphere of San Carlos he exercised enough influence to bring together Indians from hostile tribal groups. Fearing his anti-white preaching, the Americans ordered Nocadelklinny's arrest. On 30 August 1881 Col. Carr's troops, having secured the shaman's arrest, were attacked by a crowd of his followers, and the White Mountain scouts mutinied. On 1 September Apaches besieged Fort Apache; but the clamour died down, and the Indians disappeared overnight.

Crook and Geronimo

The dramatic increase in the military presence at San Carlos provoked the outbreak of Chiricahua including Juh, Chato Naiche and Geronimo. Geronimo, a shaman and warrior of the Bedonkohe band, had been hardened for war from an early age by the Mexican massacre of his family; he consequently had a particular loathing for Mexicans, whom he used to boast that he killed 'with rocks'. Through his association with Juh and his

Nednhi Apaches, who formed part of the hostile band that roamed the Sierra Madre, Geronimo had earned a fearsome reputation by 1880.

In April 1882 Juh and Geronimo secretly slipped back onto the reservation and forcefully persuaded Loco's people to flee with them. The chief of Indian police, Albert Sterling, was shot dead, and Geronimo led the group of several hundred Chiricahuas away from the agency. Pursued by troops including cavalry under Col. George Forsyth, the Apaches—supposedly protected by Geronimo's power to delay the coming of daylight—reached the Mexican border. Relaxing their vigilance, however, they stumbled into a Mexican ambush, and suffered severe casualties. Even Apaches were not infallible.

In September 1882 Gen. Crook resumed command of the Department of Arizona, and listened to the grievances of the San Carlos Apaches. He stationed a cavalry unit at San Carlos to prevent the hostiles sneaking back, and organised his mule trains and five companies of White Mountain Apache scouts to pursue the raiders. His force of 50 soldiers was dwarfed by the presence of 00 Apache scouts, who wore scarlet headbands to

A posed photograph of a US scouting party in the field. Note the gauntlets, sacred feather war-medicine caps, and the crouching position of the front Apache scout. They are armed with Springfield rifles. (Arizona State Museum, University of Arizona)

identify themselves as they crossed the border into Mexico—which was now permitted under a new 'hot pursuit' agreement between the Mexicans and Americans.

In March 1883 the hostiles unleashed lightning raids into Mexico, south-east Arizona and New Mexico. On 1 May 1883 Crook's Sierra Madre Expedition commenced; and, guided by a scout known as Peaches who had lived with the hostiles, the force followed the raiders as they recoiled into their Sierra Madre fortress. The scouts, under Capt. Emmett Crawford, scaled the rugged range in advance of the main party, guided by refuse from old camps, and by signs of dances. They surrounded the hostiles' main mountain camp as best they could and captured it, killing nine people, while most of the renegade men were away raiding.

Impressed by Crook, and feeling that they could trust him, the renegade Apaches surrendered after Geronimo had made three long parleys. Crook then escorted over 325 Apaches back to San Carlos, but

Geronimo and his band of hostiles shortly before their surrender to Crook, 1886: excellent reference of Apache costume actually worn in the field. Note the variety of weapons and headbands, typical face-paint, and unusual war-cap; and the costume and spy-glass case of Cochise's son Naiché on the far right. (Arizona State Museum, University of Arizona)

accepted Geronimo's word that he would come in himself when he had gathered all his people. To many people's surprise, Geronimo repaid Crook's trust, arriving in March 1884 (driving a huge herd of stolen Mexican cattle, which were duly confiscated). Such hardened renegades as Chihuahua, Nana, Loco, Chato and Geronimo were now on the reservation; while the irreconcilable Juh had drowned during the autumn of 1883.

In May 1885, however, following a bout of illegal tiswin-drinking, Geronimo, fearing his rumoured arrest, bolted from San Carlos accompanied by Chihuahua; Naiche, son of Cochise; Nana; and Mangas, son of Mangas Coloradas. A telegram warning Crook of the escape was filed, and failed to reach him. Chihuahua split from the other Apaches, and was pursued by Lt. Davis into Mexico. Crook meanwhile placed cavalry along the border at all water holes, and organised a pursuit by Apache scouts as Geronimo again sought the refuge of the Sierra Madre. In January Crawford's scouts captured the hostiles' horses and provisions, and opened negotiations with Geronimo; but Crawford was then shot and killed by Mexican scalp-hunters, a murder for which his scouts sought furious vengeance.

Threatened by American and Mexican soldiers, and relentlessly harassed by the scouts, on 25 March 1886 Geronimo parleyed with Crook, and with

Chato and Alchise who had accompanied the general. On condition that they would be allowed to return to their families after two years imprisonment in the East, Geronimo said: 'Once I moved about like the wind. Now I surrender to you—and that is all'. The War Department reneged on Crook's terms, however, their demand for unconditional surrender placing Crook in an impossible position. Thirty-nine hostile Chiricahuas under Geronimo and Naiche had meanwhile fled once more after being supplied with whiskey by a trader. At the suggestion that his Apache scouts had colluded in the affair, Crook resigned in disgust on 1 April and was replaced by Brig.-Gen. Nelson ('Bear Coat') Miles. The 77 fugitive Chiricahuas who had surrendered were entrained for Fort Marion, Oklahoma and arrived on 13 April 1886.

Miles unleashed hundreds of scouts and 5,000 soldiers—about one-third of the army's strength on the frontier—after 20 warriors and 13 women. Ultimately, two scouts secured a parley; and on 4 September 1886 Geronimo surrendered for the last time. In the course of 1885–86 his band had inflicted some 95 casualties on the US Army and American civilians, and killed an unknown number of Mexicans; Geronimo's losses are thought to have totalled 13, few if any to direct US Army action. He and his warriors were sent to Fort Pickens, Florida in 1886, while their families went to Fort Marion. Under Miles, even the peaceful Chiricahuas were dispatched to the overcrowded Florida forts, 381 being sent in September 1886. Among those held there were Crook's loyal scouts, who had been promised a payment of ten ponies rather than incarceration.

In 1887 a loyal scout known as the Apache Kid was imprisoned for shooting the killer of his father, but escaped and eluded capture until his reported death in the Sierra Madre from tuberculosis in 1894. The luckless Arivaipa Eskiminzin, was accused of aiding the Apache Kid and, without Crook's protection, was also exiled from his prospering fields to Florida.

The Chiricahua were moved to Mt. Vernon Barracks, Alabama, in 1887 and 1888, though this was little improvement. In 1894 they were moved to Fort Sill, Oklahoma, where Geronimo died on 17 February 1909. The Western Apache groups remained at San Carlos Reservation, while the Jicarilla were granted a reservation in Rio Arriba in 1880. The Mescalero finally received title to their lands on the eastern slopes of the White and Sacramento Mountains in 1922. The Lipan had moved to the Mescalero Reservation in 1903. In 1913 the Chiricahuas in Oklahoma were finally given their freedom: 84 of them continued to farm their lands at Fort Sill, while 187 returned at last to the South-West's Apacheria, and lived on the Mescalero Reservation.

The Plates

1: Apache Gan Dancers

The costume of the *gan* dancers invoked the supernatural power of the Mountain Spirits, principally for curative ceremonies and to ward off evil; and was based upon the presiding shaman's vision of the *gan*, and each dancer's personal designs.

1: Western Apache gan dancer

A bandana holds in place his black-dyed cloth hood, which has holes cut for eyes and mouth, plus false 'eyes' of silver buttons. Breathing was clearly very difficult, and the *gan* dancers required frequent rests. Above the mask, and painted with sacred designs, is the yucca rack, called 'horns' by the Apache in reference to the *gans'* rôle as protectors of game. Like the painted, slatted yucca wands held in the hands, it is very elaborate, as was typical among the Western Apache. His body-paint, and arm-trailers of rawhide and red cloth with eagle feathers, are further symbols of power. He wears traditional *gan* costume of fringed buckskin kilt with tin cone janglers and brass bells, beaded knee-high moccasins with disc toes, and a wide leather belt decorated with silver conches, brass tacks and bells.

A2: Mescalero Apache gan dancer

He wears a dyed cloth mask with silver button 'eyes', a bandana, and a painted rack topped with a dyed eagle 'fluffy'. The tin disc at the centre of the rack symbolises Sun; the wooden drops at the ends of the horns, Rain; and the paint designs on rack, wands, mask and body are symbolic of such supernaturals as Stars, Lightning and the Four Directions. Streamers of cloth and eagle feathers

A 1900s photograph of an old Apache woman fiercely fleshing a buckskin, included more for evocative atmosphere than costume detail. (Arizona State Museum, University of Arizona)

swirl from his arms. He wears knee-high buckskin, disc-toe moccasins, a buckskin kilt decorated with tin cones and beadwork, and a tacked leather belt.

A3: Chiricahua Apache gan dancer

His traditional mask of buckskin—dyed, painted, and held in place with a cloth bandana—has a cluster of rattlesnake rattles (here hidden at the back). The typical painted, slatted rack, topped with dyed eagle 'fluffies', has wooden pendants symbolising rain, and turkey feathers at its base invoking the Mountain Spirits. His arms are adorned with red flannel trailers and brass bells, and his body with sacred paint designs. He carries typically simple Chiricahua wands; and wears a leather belt with silver conches, and knee-high buckskin disc-toe moccasins. His fringed buckskin kilt is decorated with tin pendants, and cut to create ornate fringes below the belt.

A young Apache woman wearing a traditional costume of necklaces and painted buckskin blouse, with fringing, beadwork and tin cone pendants, worn over a cotton skirt. Apache baskets and a pitch-covered water jar comprise the studio props. (Arizona State Museum, University of Arizona)

B: Chiricahua Apache (based upon contemporary photographs of Geronimo's hostile band, circa 1886):

B1: Chiricahua warrior

An archetypal Apache warrior: he wears a cloth headband, white-stripe war paint, bead necklace, neckerchief tied with a silver conch, cotton shirt, loose cotton drawers, breechclout, and boot-length buckskin moccasins bound above the calf. Over a buttoned waistcoat of corduroy he wears a war medicine thong of shell and beads slung from his right shoulder and holding a beaded 'ration-ticket pouch' fringed with tin cones. Tweezers (for plucking facial hair) hang from a thong around his neck. He carries an 1873 Winchester carbine decorated with brass tacks. He has two cartridge belts; one, decorated with red paint, supports a holster which holds a 'pearl'-handled Colt double action 'Frontier' Model 1878, a thong hanging from the lanyard-ring on the butt. A buckskin serves as the horse's saddle, and the bridle is leather decorated with brass tacks and silver.

B2: Chiricahua warrior

He wears a cotton shirt, loose cotton drawers, breechclout, moccasins, cartridge belt, and a headband in distinctive folded style. His beaded necklace centres on a silver conch, and a mirror forms a part of his sacred, beaded war-medicine thong. He is armed with a .45/70 Springfield rifle.

B3: Chiricahua woman

She wears a cotton blouse and skirt, leather conch belt, beaded bracelets, and a necklace of beads and shells with conch pendant. Her face is daubed with paint; and she holds a sling—a traditional Apache weapon.

B4: Chiricahua warrior

His distinctive war-cap, with paint designs and rawhide 'ears', invokes supernatural protection in battle. He wears a heavy jacket over a cotton shirt, breechclout and moccasins, and his neckerchief threads through silver conches and is hung with beads. Armed with a .45/70 Springfield carbine, he wears a conch-belt and a cartridge-belt.

B5: Chiricahua woman

Wearing a cotton blouse and typical bead

necklaces, she has daubed across her face the white stripe considered so typical of the Chiricahua men.

B6: Chiricahua warrior

In contrast to much Mexican-influenced costume, he wears more traditional garb of headband, conch and bead necklace, moccasins, and breechclout hung over a belt—this being typically narrow at the front, long and wrapped wide at the back. He carries a lance, deerskin quiver and bow case decorated with red flannel, and a 'flop-head' club: a club encased in rawhide with a slashed section between the stone head and wooden handle, to make it flexible and to prevent the club from breaking upon impact.

C: Chiricahua Puberty Ceremony

With the sacred tipi in the background, the maiden's sponsor pushes her away to make four ritual runs, accompanied by the presiding shaman's singing. Cattail fronds—symbols of renewal—carpet the ground.

C1: Puberty rite maiden

She is dressed to represent White Painted Woman, who is invoked by the abalone shell in her beaded necklaces. The girl's ritually-prepared deerskin dress is decorated with fringing, brass buttons, tin cone pendants, and beadwork designs representing her protective supernaturals. Like the beaded deerskin disc-toe moccasins, the dress is coloured yellow to symbolise pollen, which is also smeared over the maiden's face. She wears a scratcher and drinking tube on a thong around her neck.

C2: Chiricahua puberty rite sponsor

An older woman of unquestionable reputation, she wears typical Chiricahua costume: a patterned cotton blouse, skirt, wide leather belt, moccasins, and necklaces of seeds.

C3: Chiricahua puberty rite shaman

He wears a cotton shirt, a two-string medicine thong strung with shells, beads, turquoise and *hoddentin* pouch, and a buckskin medicine hat decorated with the horns and fur of a prong-horned deer, felt symbols and tassels, paint designs and a horsehair fringe at the back (based upon an example in the Museum of the American Indian,

New York). His left hand is painted with a Sun symbol, and his right hand clutches a deer dew-claw rattle.

D: Western Apache

Wagering on games was a favourite pastime of the Apaches, and the use of rawhide playing cards adapted from Spanish decks became a distinctive Apache trait. Both men and women played such card games as 'monte'; in contrast, the men's popular 'hoop and pole' game was sacred and could not be witnessed by women.

D1: San Carlos warrior

He wears a cloth headband, under which passes a thin buckskin band war-amulet, braided into the hair and decorated with shell. His fringed buckskin war shirt is decorated with beadwork, brass tacks, and crosses and raised discs or conches of German silver. Spanish/Mexican influence is shown in the

An 1880s studio shot showing White Mountain Apache women's costume, and the man's feathered war-cap and use of blanket. (Arizona State Museum, University of Arizona)

loose white cotton drawers and striped socks, as seen in many contemporary photographs. He also wears typical Western Apache moccasins, with upturned discs on the toes; and a cloth breechclout. The Apaches were compulsive gamblers, and would even wager their metal identification tags (which Crook had introduced to distinguish between reservation and 'hostile' Indians).

D2: San Carlos warrior

He wears a patterned headband and a buckskin band war-amulet decorated with beadwork, metal plates and shells, again braided into the hair. The elaborate war-shirt, decorated with fringing, brass tacks and intricate beadwork, is worn over a

US Army officer and band of unidentified Apache scouts armed with Springfield rifles. (Arizona State Museum, University of Arizona)

patterned shirt. His jewellery consists of a bead necklace with three drops of silver discs and a silver cross; a cluster of bracelets made from beads and cowrie shells; and a collection of silver rings. He also wears cotton drawers, breechclout, disc-toe moccasins decorated with beadwork; and a reservation identification tag hanging by a chain from his necklace.

D3: Tonto warrior

He wears a breeechclout, moccasins, beaded bracelets, and a sacred medicine cord. This latter comprises four intertwined thongs of dyed buckskin strung with beads, shells, pieces of turquoise, and rattlesnake rattles, and holds a buckskin bag of *hoddentin*. Such cords might consist of one, two, three or four thongs, and were important as shamans' paraphernalia and warriors' protective amulets

His war-cap of clipped turkey and two eagle feathers imparted protection and swiftness in battle, and is based upon an example in the Musem of the American Indian, New York.

D4: Western Apache fiddle player

He wears a breechclout, cotton drawers, shirt, waistcoat, headband, neckerchief, necklace of beads and cowrie shells, and wide leather belt with silver conches. His Apache fiddle, crafted from the painted stalk of a mescal plant and played socially rather than ceremonially, was most typically found among the Western Apache. The fiddle, like the wooden bow, is strung with horsehair, and is small in comparison to those examples later made purely for trade.

D5: Western Apache woman

Wearing typical full blouse and skirt, and necklaces of trade beads and mirrors, she uses a headstrap to carry a twined burden basket. Decorated with paint designs, leather fringes and tin cone pendants, and strengthened by a rawhide base, the basket could also be hung from a horse's saddle.

D6: Western Apache shaman

The shaman wears the paraphernalia invoking his power to perform curative ceremonies. His medicine shirt, a folded buckskin rectangle with a head-hole, is painted with symbols representing his power, hung with shells, and worn over a cotton shirt. His wands, representing the Four Directions, are hung with eagle feathers and painted with designs including the Snake; this supernatural is also the central feature of his medicine hat (based upon an example in the Museum of the American Indian, New York). Other ceremonial objects are carried in his painted, fringed buckskin medicine bag.

D7: White Mountain Apache woman

She wears beaded earrings, skirt, and patterned blouse. Contemporary photographs show that both men and women wore cartridge belts, and hanging from hers is a sheath holding a butcher knife. Her hair is folded up into a leather '*nah-leen*' or hair-bow decorated with beadwork, brass tacks and long, bright ribbons, indicating that she is eligible for marriage.

D8: Western Apache woman
Wearing cotton blouse and skirt, and a necklace of beads with a mirror pendant, she demonstrates the method of carrying the cradleboard, which has protective amulets hung around the hood.

E: Mescalero Apache:
E1: Mounted Mescalero warrior
He wears a waistcoat, cotton shirt, fringed leggings decorated with brass studs, beaded moccasins of the Plains type, and a blanket around his waist. The buckskin war-cap—decorated with a checke[r] beadwork browband, beadwork top, a bea[d] wrapped horsehair pendant and dyed feathers— has an unusual Plains-like trailer of eagle feathe[rs] on a buckskin strip decorated with painted bird an[d] animal symbols (after an example in the Museum [of] the American Indian, New York). He wea[rs] typically long silver earrings; and carries a painte[d] medicine shield, and a fringed quiver and bowcas[e] decorated with cloth and beadwork, made from th[e] prized skin of a mountain lion. The horse wears [a] captured US Army bridle decorated with bras[s] tacks.

E2: Mescalero warrior
He wears a fringed buckskin shirt decorated wit[h] painted symbols and tin cone pendants; clot[h] wrapped around his waist; fringed moccasin[s] embellished with beadwork and tin cone pendant[s]

Geronimo and his band *en route* to a Florida prison camp, 1886. (Robin May Collection)

nd beaded, fringed buckskin leggings, based upon pair in the Museum of the American Indian, New 'ork. His open-topped fur turban, typical of the Mescalero, is decorated with cloth, pearl buttons, luffies' and an eagle feather. A bear claw hangs om a thong around his neck; he carries a typically ong-bladed lance decorated with cloth, beadwork nd feathers, and a painted medicine shield.

3: Mounted Mescalero woman with cradleboard
oth the cradleboard, hung with several protective mulets, and the woman's painted, beaded and ringed buckskin dress are based upon examples in he Museum of the American Indian, New York.

: Jicarilla Apache:
1: Jicarilla warrior
He wears Plains-type beaded moccasins, heavily ringed and beaded skin leggings, and a typically ong trade-cloth breechclout. His buckskin shirt vith long fringes and beaded panels, and his choker f leather studded with brass tacks and studs and ung with beads and shells, are based upon xamples in the Museum of the American Indian, New York. He wears a Plains-type eagle feather pright-bonnet, with beaded browband; and eaded hair-tubes typical of the Jicarilla. He has nudged white war paint on to his cheeks, and arries a 'flop-head' club.

2: Jicarilla warrior
single eagle feather in his hair, this warrior too vears beaded hair-tubes, with distinctive face-aint, and hair-pipe bone choker and drop arrings. He holds an eagle feather fan. An otter kin is worn over the front of a fringed buckskin hirt, and a long breechclout with beaded cloth ggings and moccasins complete the costume.

3: Jicarilla woman
Over a cloth dress with added patterned hem she vears a typical, beautifully-beaded cape. Her ggings are beaded, but her moccasins, in common ith most Jicarilla women's, are plain. Her hair is ed with yarn; and she wears face-paint, hair-pipe one chokers, and necklaces of hair-pipe bone, eads and silver conches. She carries a basket, and vears the distinctive Jicarilla broad leather belt ecorated with a brass chain and tacks.

Oliver Otis Howard, the one-armed, bible-toting 'praying general' who implemented Grant's 'peace policy' in the South-West. (Robin May Collection)

G: Apache Scouts
While US Army Apache scouts were issued with various uniforms, they usually wore a combination of Army clothing and traditional costume. The scouts here examine the dying embers of a camp fire, an abandoned 'wickiup' in the background.

G1: Apache Scout
He wears a US Army dress helmet, which was later—in 1890—issued to the scouts with the addition of a crossed arrows badge mounted on the staff plate. (It was issued as part of an official full dress uniform for the US Indian Scouts, whose branch-of-service colour became white piped with red.) The five-button fatigue jacket, trousers and boots are all Army issue. He has a tacked leather choker; leather gauntlets, first issued to mounted troops in about 1885; and an 1873 Winchester carbine.

G2: Apache Scout
His costume consists of Apache moccasins, breech-clout, bead and shell bracelets; and an issue Army

blouse turned inside out for the sake of the grey lining's lower visibility. He wears a cartridge-belt supporting a butcher knife in a tacked sheath, and holds a Springfield carbine. His 'keyhole' identity tag's shape and number reveal his position in band and tribe and his rôle as a scout, in accordance with Crook's 1873 'tagging' policy. Supernatural power is invoked by the beaded medicine string, and the striking buckskin war-cap adorned with paint and owl feathers, based upon an example in the Museum of the American Indian, New York.

Three warriors, probably Tonto Apache, wearing traditional costume including distinctive war-caps, and carrying lance, bow and arrow, and Springfield rifle. (Robin May Collection)

G3: First Sergeant of Scouts

He bears the stripes of his rank (at this date, i cavalry yellow) on a five-button fatigue jacket, an wears the red headband which was considere regulation for scouts but which was actually fa from universal. He is armed with a Springfiel carbine.

G4: Apache Scout

He has cut the seat from his loose cotton drawers t create leggings, worn with moccasins, cotto breechclout, patterned shirt, waistcoat, and beade bracelets. He is armed with an 1873 'trapdoo Springfield .45/70 rifle, and wears the Mil

artridge-belt. His buckskin war-cap is decorated with beadwork and eagle feathers, and based upon an example in the Museum of the American Indian.

5: Apache Scout

He wears knee-high moccasins, cotton drawers, breechclout, typical striped trade shirt and cartridge-belt. The more incongruous influence from white culture is shown in the binocular case, white man's hat with upturned brim, and neatly knotted neck-tie.

Chato, possibly photographed in 1886—the Chiricahua leader who frequently fled the reservation to raid with Geronimo, but who in 1886 helped Crook to agree a parley with Geronimo's renegade band. Chato was one of the Chiricahuas who settled on the Mescalero Reservation in 1913. (Robin May Collection)

Bibliography

Adams, *Geronimo* (New English Library)

American Indian Art Magazine

Arizona Highways

Bahti, *Southwestern Indian Ceremonials* (KC)

Bahti, *Southwestern Indian Tribes* (KC)

Ball, *In The Days of Victorio* (Corgi)

Barrett, *Geronimo, His Own Story* (Abacus)

Bleeker, *The Apache Indians* (Dobson)

Bourke, *On The Border With Crook* (Time Life)

Brown, *Bury My Heart At Wounded Knee* (Pan)

Conn, *Robes of White Shell and Sunrise* (Denver Art Museum)

Cremony, *Life Among The Apaches* (Bison)

Davis, *The Truth About Geronimo* (Yale)

Debo, *Geronimo: The Man, His Time, His Place* (University of Oklahoma)

Forbes, *Apache, Navajo and Spaniard* (University of Oklahoma)

Handbook of North American Indians – 10 – Southwest (Smithsonian)

Hook, *The American Plains Indians* (Osprey)

Katcher, *The American Indian Wars 1860–1890* (Osprey)

Mails, *The People Called Apache* (Promontory)

May, *Indians* (Bison Books)

Mooney, *Calendar History of the Kiowa Indians* (Smithsonian)

Peterson and Elman, *The Great Guns* (Grosset and Dunlap)

Scherer, *Indians* (Bonanza)

Schmitt and Brown, *Fighting Indians of the West* (Charles Scribner's Sons)

Severn, *Conquering The Frontiers* (Foundation)

Sonnichsen, *The Mescalero Apaches* (University of Oklahoma)

Swanton, *The Indian Tribes of North America* (Smithsonian)

The Old West: The Great Chiefs (Time Life)

The Old West: The Indians (Time Life)

The Old West: The Scouts (Time Life)

The Old West: The Soldiers (Time Life)

The World of The American Indian (National Geographic)

Utley, *Bluecoats and Redskins* (Purnell)

Utley, *The History of The Indian Wars* (Mitchell Beazley)

Waldman and Braun, *The Atlas of The North American Indian* (Facts on File)

With Eagle Glance (Museum of The American Indian)

Worcester, *The Apaches, Eagles of the Southwest* (University of Oklahoma)

Articles

Chappell, *United States Scouts.*

Granfelt, *Apache Indian Identification Tags.*

Hoseney, *United States Scouts, 1890.*

Jacobsen, Jr, *The Uniform of the Indian Scouts.*

Lewis and Magruder, *Captain Crawford's Battalion of Apache Scouts, 1885.*

Notes sur les planches en couleur

A Les danseurs *Gan* invoquaient le pouvoir surnaturel des esprits de la montagne lors de cérémonies curatives et pour écarter les mauvais esprits. Les éléments courants du costume étaient la cagoule marquée de faux 'yeux' par des boutons et une 'crémaillère' peinte, comme des andouillers; un kilt en peau de daim, à franges et des mocassins hauts; peinture sur le corps et banderoles d'étoffe et plumes sur les bras; et baguettes divinatoires complexes, semblables à la crémaillère sur la tête. Les détails dépendaient des visions du chaman qui présidait et de l'inspiration personnelle de chaque danseur. Les danses étaient des événements de grande importance; l'effort physique était énorme et prolongé et les peines en cas d'erreurs graves.

B (D'après des photos de la bande de Géronimo en 1886). **B1** Un archétype de guerrier apache: bandeau en tissu, rayure de peinture blanche, collier de perles, tour de cou attaché par un *conch* en argent; chemise de cotton et caleçons larges, bande-culotte et mocassins hauts. Il a ajouté un gilet en velours côtelé et une lanière de cuir de 'magie de guerre' décorée de coquillages et perles est portée en bandoulière sur l'épaule gauche et contient une bourse pour ses tickets de rationnement de la réserve indienne; notez la décoration cônique en étain. Des pinces pour enlever les poils du visage pendaient au cou. Les armes comprennent une carabine Winchester de 1873 avec décoration d'argent et un révolver Colt de 1878. L'on verra à nouveau sur d'autres clichés plusieurs éléments semblables. **B2** Notez le bandeau replié distinctement; un miroir sur une lanière de cuir de 'magie de guerre'; et un fusil Springfield de .45/70. **B3** Notez la peinture et la fronde — une arme traditionnelle apache. **B4** Des coiffures de guerre décorées de manières variées étaient courantes, ayant une valeur protectrice rituelle. **B5** La rayure de peinture blanche était une caractéristique Chiricahua, mais elle n'était pas particulière à cette tribu. **B6** Un habit plus traditionnel et moins influencé par les styles mexicains; notez la lance, le carquois et l'étui de l'arc en peau de daim ainsi que la massue avec section flexible sous la tête.

C1 Habillée pour représenter la personnalité mystique de la 'Femme peinte en blanc', cette jeune fille est richement parée d'articles et de couleurs rituels—le jaune par ex. représentant le pollen sacré. Sa 'marraine', **C2**, une femme d'un certain âge à la vertu incontestable, est vêtue plus simplement. **C3** Le costume du chaman comprend une lanière double de cuir de 'magie' avec un sac de pollen et une coiffure en peau de daim décorée de cornes d'antilocapre. Il tient à la main droite une crécelle, et un symbole solaire est peint sur sa main gauche.

D Les hommes et les femmes jouaient à de nombreux jeux de cartes avec des 'cartes' de cuir copiées à l'origine sur les premiers modèles espagnols. **D1** Notez l'amulette de guerre fixée autour de la tête sous le bandeau; chemise de guerre en peau de daim; chaussettes rayées copiées sur des modèles mexicains et espagnols; mocassins caractéristiques de l'Apache de l'Ouest avec 'disques' pour les orteils. **D2** est largement similaire. **D3** Notez le 'cordon de magie' à quatre cordes, une amulette protectrice; et une coiffure de guerre composée de plumes de dinde fixées dont deux plumes d'aigle donnant de la célérité lors du combat. **D4** L'instrument de musique, fabriqué à partir de la tige peinte d'une plante à *mescal* avec des cordes en crin de cheval, se jouait avec un arc de bois; son emploi était plutôt social que rituel. **D5** Chemisier et jupe, complets, caractéristiques; panier suspendu sur une bande enroulée autour de la tête. **D6** 'Coiffure de sorcier', vêtement en peau de daim peint, porté sur une chemise, 'sac à magie' et baguettes divinatoires forment le costume rituel des cérémonies curatives. **D7** Les hommes et les femmes portaient des ceintures-cartouchières. Ses cheveux sont noués par une barrette indiquant qu'elle est éligible au marriage. **D8** Notez le berceau suspendu, avec des amulettes protectrices.

E1 Notez certains éléments de costume semblables aux styles de l'Indien de la Plaine: jambières, mocassins, couverture portée jusqu'à la ceinture et la décoration sur la coiffure. Le carquois à frange et l'étui à arc sont en fourrure de cougar très recherchée; la bride est un modèle de l'*US Army* qui a été capturé. **E2** La longue lance et le 'turban' en fourrure laissant le sommet de la tête découvert sont caractéristiques de l'Indien Mescalero. **E3** Les exemples de vêtement en peau de daim à frange et le berceau sont conservés au *Museum of the American Indian*, New York.

F1 Notez la longue bande-culotte; Modèles de mocassins et jambières de l'Indien de la Plaine; Coiffure de guerre de l'Indien de la Plaine; os creux décorés de perles servant de parure de chevelure à l'Indien Jicarilla. **F2** Les os creux utilisés pour parer la chevelure et la peinture sur le visage sont caractéristiques de l'Indien Jicarilla. **F3** La belle cape et les jambières sont décorées de perles; mais les mocassins sont simples dans cette tribu. La ceinture large et décorée est aussi caractéristique; et notez la parure de cou en os creux.

G Des mélanges personnels de costume indien et de pièces d'uniforme de *l'US Army* étaient caractéristiques. Le casque de l'armée, de grande tenue, de **G1** est un prix personnel—ces casques ont été distribués plus tard, en 1890, et faisaient partie d'un uniforme de grande tenue complet prescrit pour les *US Indian Scouts*, bien qu'avec des signes distinctifs différents. La veste, le pantalon, les bottes et les gants ont été distribués par l'armée. Seule la veste, qui a été retournée pour en dissimuler trahit le costume de **G2** qui est par ailleurs entièrement aborigène. **G3** Les insigne de grade sont jaunes dans l'*US Cavalry* à ce moment-là, le bandeau rouge était une identification officielle pour les scouts, mais était souvent mis de côté. **G4, G5** Mélanges caractéristiques de vêtements et d'équipement d'homme blanc et aborigènes.

Fabtafeln

A Gan-Tänzer beschwören die übermenschlichen Kräfte der Berggeister Heilungszeremonien und um böse Einflüsse abzuwehren. Gemeinsame Elemen in den Kostümen waren die Hauben mit falschen Knopfaugen und ein aufgemaltes Geweih, ein gefranster Wildlederrock und hohe Mokkasins, Körperbemalung und Bänder aus Stoff und Federn an den Armen; dazu kam komplexe Zauberstäbe, ähnlich wie das Gestell auf dem Kopf. Deta orientierten sich an den Visionen, die der vorhergehende Schamane erlebt hat sowie an den individuellen Erfahrungen der einzelnen Tänzer. Die Tänze war sehr wichtige Veranstaltungen, sie verlangten eine enorme physische Anstre gung, und Fehler wurden schwer bestraft.

B (Nach Fotos von Geronimos Bande aus dem Jahr 1886.) **B1** Archetypisch Apachenkrieger: Kopfband aus Stoff, weisse Farbenstreifen, Perlenhalsbai halstuch mit silbernem Conch befestigt, Baumwollhemd und weite Unterhose Gesässschurz und hohe Mokkasins. Er trägt ausserdem eine Kordweste und 'Kriegszauber'—Band mit Muschel—und Perlenschmuck über den linke Schulter, an der ein Beutel für seine Reservations-Verpflegungskarten befest ist; man beachte die Zinnkegelverzierung. Eine Pinzette, mit der er sei Gesichtshaare entfernt, hängt um seinen Hals. Die Waffen sind im Winches 1873 Karabiner mit Messingnagelbesatz und ein Colt 1878 Revolver. Viele die Details finden sich auch auf anderen Tafeln. **B2** Man beachte das auffä gefaltete Kopfband, den Spiegel am 'Kriegszauber'—Band und das 0.45/ Springfield Gewehr. **B3** Man beachte die Bemalung und die Schleuder, ei traditionelle Apachenwaffe. **B4** Kriegerische Kopfbedeckungen waren i verschiedenen Verzierungen weit verbreitet und galten als rituelle Schutzvo richtung. **B5** Die weissen Farbstreifen waren typisch für die Chirichua, aber ni auf diesen Stamm allein beschränkt. **B6** Traditionellere Tracht mit weni mexikanischen Einflüssen; man beachte die Lanze, den Köcher aus Rehhaut u den Bogenhalter sowie den beweglichen Haarknoten.

C1 Dieses Mädchen, gekleidet als die mystische 'Weissbemalte Frau', ist r rituellen Schmuckstücken und Farben reich verziert; die Farbe gelb repräsenti beispielsweise heiligen Pollen. Ihre 'Mäzenin', **C2**, eine ältere Frau v unangreifbarer Tugend, ist schlichter gekleidet. **C3** Das Kostüm des Schman enthält ein zweiteiliges Zauberband mit einem Pollenbeutel und e Kopfbedeckung aus Rehhaut mit den Hörnern einer Gabelantilope. In rechten Hand hält er eine Klapper, die linke ist mit einem Sonnensymbol bema

D Männer und Frauen spielten verschiedene Kartenspiele mit ledernen 'Kart nach frühen spanischen Vorbildern. **D1** Man beachte das Kriegsamulett, un dem Stoffband um den Kopf gewickelt, das Kriegshemd aus Wildleder, gestreiften Socken nach spanischen und mexikanischen Vorbildern und die westlichen Apachen typischen Mokkasins mit rundem Vorderteil. **D2** weitgehend identisch. **D3** Man beachte das vierteilige 'Zauber'-Band, Schutzamulett, und die Kriegskopfbedeckung aus gestutzten Truthahnfede mit zwei Adlerfedern, die in der Schlacht Schnelligkeit verleihen sollten. **D4** I Musikinstrument, hergestellt auf dem bemalten Stamm der Mescal-Pflanze u Pferdehaar, wurde mit einem hölzernen Bogen gespielt und für gesellige s rituelle Anlässe benutzt. **D5** Typische vollständige Bluse mit Rock, der Kc hängt an einem Kopfriemen. **D6** 'Zauberhut', Oberhemd aus bemalt Wildleder, 'Zaubertasche' und Zauberstab bilden Bestandteile des Ritualk tüms bei Heilungszeremonien. **D7** Männer und Frauen trugen Patronengür Der Haarknoten der Frau zeigt an, dass sie im heiratsfähigen Alter ist. **D8** beachte die übergeworfene Krippe mit Schutzamuletten.

E1 Einige Elemente der Tracht erinnern an die Bekleidung der Plains-Indian Beinschutz, Mokkasins, Hüfttuch und die Verzierung der Kopfbedeckung. I gefranste Köcher und Bogenhalter sind mit dem kostbaren Pelz eines Kugu hergestellt; die Zügel wurde von der US Army erbeutet. **E2** Die lange Lanze u der feine Pelzturban sind typisch für die Mescaleros. **E3** Exemplare gefransten Wildlederbekleidung und der Krippe sind im New Yorker Museum the American Indian erhalten geblieben.

F1 Man beachte den langen Gasässschurz, Mokkassins und Beinschutz im Plai Stil, Kriegskopfbedeckung nach Plains-Vorbild und perlenbesetzte Ha röhrchen der Jicarilla. **F2** Die Haarröhrchen und die Gesichtsbemalung typisch für die Jicarilla. **F3** Der schöne Mantelkragen und der Beinschutz sind Perlenknöpfen besetzt, aber Mokkassins sind in diesem Stamm schmucklos. I breite, verzierte Gürtel ist ebenfalls charakteristisch; man beachte Haarverzierung durch Knochenröhrchen.

G Individuelle Mischungen aus indianischen Trachten und Teilen der US Arn Uniformen waren verbreitet. **G1** Der Helm der vollen Army-Uniform ist e individuelle Auszeichnung; solche Helme wurden ab 1890 als offizie Bestandteil der US Indian Scout-Uniform ausgegeben, allerdings mit ande Abzeichen. Jacke, Hosen, Stiefel und Handschuhe stammen von der US Arn Nur eine nach aussen umgekehrt getragene Jacke verrät im übrig authentische Indianertracht von **G2**. **G3** Rangabzeichen im Gelb der Cavalry; das rote Kopfband war das offizielle Erkennungszeichen der Sco wurde aber oft nicht getragen. **G4, G5** Typische Mischung aus Bekleidungs—u Ausrüstungsgegenständen der Weissen und Indianer.